MW00896045

GETTING
A
HEAD

touring the world as
a giant dancing bear

DANIEL FALK

I want to Drink
Your Cider.

DAN FALL

Copyright 2014 Daniel Falk
Published by TheGreatRobotPress

Cover Design: Trevor Campbell
trevorcampbelldesign.com

Getting a Head originally appeared on McSweeney's Internet
Tendency
www.mcsweeneys.net/tendency

Print Edition License Notes
All rights reserved. No part of this book may be reproduced in any
form or by any means without the permission of the author, except
for the inclusion of brief quotations in a review.

ISBN 978-1-304-85032-4

ACKNOWLEDGEMENTS

Though I must ultimately take responsibility for what I hath wrought, there are people who should, at the very least, be held partly accountable. My editors at McSweeney's, John Warner and Chris Monks, have been abetting me since this book's original column form. My mother has been enabling me this behaviour with encouragement and unconditional love for my entire life. My father is responsible for brainwashing me to love writing *AND* to love theatre ever since I was an innocent little boy. And the biggest offender of all, my wife, Sarah... She's the one who got me the gig touring around the world as a giant dancing bear to begin with. She's the one who kept me just sane enough to emerge from the bear head with enough sanity to write at least semi-coherently about it. She's the one who's loved me enough to dig me out of holes, prop me up, and kick me in the ass as necessary. She'd also be my getaway driver if she knew how to drive.

TABLE OF CONTENTS

Into the Head   1

The Stump Complex   5

The Day the Fan Stood Still   9

Bear's Guide to Hotel Cookery   14

Remembering Bird   17

That Which Cannot Be Named   21

Captain Unicycle's Blog   24

Do You Know Who I Am?   27

Buy the Merch   32

Fart Protocol   35

Dumpster Diving in Marseille   39

Nine Hours of Trivial Pursuit   43

Shooting Star is Dead Inside   47

The Disappearing Rabbit Trick   52

Lame Bus/Party Bus   57

Squished Fox   61

Space Invader Safari   65

The Missus   69

Out of the Head   74

INTO THE HEAD

Backstage, Lloydminster, Saskatchewan, Canada.

I stare into the tangle of straps in the empty hole of what will soon be my giant bear head. Is this really what I'm about to do? Am I sure I don't just want to get some student loans and go back to school and become a teacher or something? No... no more debt. That's why I'm here to begin with: to get myself out of the hole I'd dug for myself by producing a play I'd written. I'm here for the money. I'm putting on this giant bear head and dancing around to pre-recorded voice-overs for the money.

The rumble of hundreds of parents asking their hundreds children if they're sure they don't need to pee one last time penetrates the heavy red curtain. Sweat already streams down my back inside the thick fur of my costume; a costume in which I am trapped, my mittened hands unable to grasp the zipper to free myself.

The houselights dim under the curtain. Unlike grown up audiences that immediately hush when the lights go dark, an audience of children just get louder until their enthusiasm is squashed by their accompanying adults. Put the head on, I tell myself. Get in the head. I close my eyes and when I reopen them, the world is dark and sound is muffled. I am in the head. My own voice is oddly close, and all other sound is oddly distant. I struggle for a few moments with the straps that keep the head from popping off and ruining children's lives before I manage to get them clipped together, pinching the skin under my jaw.

My only window to the outside world is a few inches of black mesh that covers the back of the bear head's constant idiotic, open-mouthed smile. My girlfriend (dressed as "The Spirit of Christmas Fairy") approaches, looks up into my mouth hole and wishes me a good show.

I tell her I can't see shit.

She assures me I'll be fine, then takes her place in the wings. What does she know, anyway? She's not in one of these stupid heads. How did I let her talk me into this?

I'm jostled from behind and stumble forward. I turn, but can only see the lower half of the giant rabbit who bumped into me, untangling some tinsel from around her legs. I lean back as far as I can to get a view of the rabbit's face. The rabbit leans back to get a look into mine and an unfamiliar voice apologizes. I apologize back for some reason. An assemblage of other animals ready themselves next to us in the wings.

Beaver steps in front of my field of vision. He puts his hand on my shoulder and says something in a very serious sounding tone. As his voice had to pass through his giant Beaver head, out into space, and then into my giant Bear head, however, the only words I understood were, "Hey, don't forget to..."

"Don't forget to what?"

"That's right. Have a great show!" And with that he was gone —running on stage to the gleeful screams of hundreds of children.

Dammit, I thought, *I'm going to kill someone out there.*

The veterans of working in those heads had a preternatural

ability to know where everyone else was on stage. I managed to make it through the big ensemble numbers by keeping my hands in front of me the entire time. Whenever I ended up in the wrong spot, or started exiting to the wrong wing, one of them would gently guide me in the right direction—and by "gently guide," I mean shove.

Sweating, heart pounding, and out of breath, I imagined the bored faces of the parents in the audience having to sit through this ridiculous show. I hated myself for taking the job. I hated my girlfriend for talking me into it. I hated everyone from the production side who was responsible for putting these shows up. But most of all, I hated the whiny children and weak-willed parents who spent so much money on its over priced merchandise.

The next song ended with a big spin, which my flagging energy had caused me to unwittingly under-do. I couldn't see that I was facing the wrong direction, so when I turned to march off stage during the applause, I was actually headed directly downstage, into the audience. An odd hush fell over the crowd, immediately after which I fell into the audience. Thankfully a gap between the stage and the front row prevented any children from being crushed by a giant dancing bear. I clambered back to my feet, collected what dignity I had left (which didn't take long, because there was none), found the stairs onto the stage and slunk off into the wings.

Backstage, Rabbit, Fox, Turtle, and Beaver were howling with laughter, which really worked because those characters had the same idiotic, open-mouthed smiles plastered on their characters' heads as mine. I made it through the rest of the show, thankful that the giant head covered the humiliation that would have otherwise been transparently displayed on my face.

After the curtain fell on the last number, I ripped the head off and made my way to the dressing room. I collapsed on a seat and stared at myself in a mirror. *Really? This is really what I've become?* The rest of the male cast members entered the dressing room joking about my fall. I accepted the ribbing with an outward good nature until they moved on to other topics. I stuffed my furry costume up into a purple canvass bag, and shoved the head into its massive box. Two more months of this tour. I sat back in my chair and pretended to play with my phone while the boys finished packing up their costumes and made their way out. A few minutes later the road manager poked his ever toque-covered head in the room.

"Hey, Bear! You got some fan mail!"

He dropped a hand coloured picture of my character in front of me. At the bottom was scrawled a name and the message, "I love you Bear!" I felt like crying. I felt like laughing. But most of all, I felt like an idiot. I had gauged my validity as a performer off the looks of a few bored parents when right next to them were enraptured children. What I was doing meant something to that child.

Though I lost the picture itself (somewhere between Fort McMurray and Fresno), the image of it stayed with me the rest of the tour. And every time I felt like I was going to die in that costume, or felt like killing one of my cast-mates or felt like my bladder would rupture on one of our epic twelve-hour drives across the rocky mountains, I remembered that every town we performed in there was some little girl out there who loved Bear, and I better make damn sure I don't walk off the stage and crush her to death.

THE STUMP COMPLEX

Few industries are as susceptible to downturns in the economy than live theatre—and when we're talking about live theatre for children, it can be especially bad. Most parents will grab any excuse they can to not have to take their screaming/urinating/puking kid to a show the kid's probably going to cry the whole way through anyway.

In one such time of proverbial belt-tightening, the Children's Theatre Company was putting together a show about an entirely different dancing ursine protagonist than my future role. The show required the construction of a simple animatronic: a magical moving tree stump that needed to slide from one side of the stage to the other. But before the mechanical components had been built, a bookkeeper made a startling discovery: the cost of weekly salary, per diem, and nightly hotels for an additional performer was actually cheaper than the cost of building and installing the animatronic. And so it was decided to put a human being into the stump.

And the Stump Complex was born.

The original Stump was a long-time member of the company, and a very skilled dancer/choreographer in her own right. There wasn't anything else available, so she accepted the role of Stump, unaware of the damage that a playing prop dead tree could have on the human mind. To some it would appear as a dream job: a ridiculously easy task for the same pay scale as anyone else on the tour.

All Stump had to do was slide across the stage, whereupon the children in the audience would scream "LOOK BEHIND YOU!!" The Little Girl character (my future wife)[1] would look at the side where the Stump had been, not see it, then ask the boys and girls what they were talking about. Then Stump would move back to its original place and the kids would scream again, but when the Little Girl looked at the other side, again, the Stump wasn't there.

Hilarious, right?

That single action is what comprised Stump's entire workload. Stump spent close to a half hour sitting on stage waiting for her moment in the spotlight, and then another half hour waiting for the curtain to close afterwards. This gave Stump up to three hours each day (one hour per show, three shows per day) during which she had nothing else to do but reflect on the choices she'd made in life that lead her to be where she was now, trapped inside a fake tree made out of plastic, plaster and papier-mâché.

At the end of the show, Stump's cast-mates would emerge from their animal costumes drenched in sweat, exhausted, and hungry. Stump, on the other hand, would emerge dry, well-rested, and utterly neurotic.

Stump was normally an instigator of on-the-road good times. Looking for someone with whom to tear up Bourbon Street? Need some company getting lost on the trails in Banff? Want someone to

---

1 As an aside I should clarify that I did not marry a little girl. She specializes in playing little girls—she's made a career out of playing Anne Frank in a variety of stage adaptations of her eponymous diary. This is slightly ironic as she would go on to marry someone who's made a career playing Nazis—a somewhat unfortunate type-cast.

get drunk with you on Two Buck Chuck from Trader Joe's? Stump-before-stump was always game. Stump-during-stump on the other hand was more likely to make her hotel roommate uncomfortable by crying in the shower.

One night in Thunder Bay, or Duluth, or wherever, Stump wobbled and fell over. Little Girl turned around, and called out "TIIIIIIMBER!"—an awfully clever ad lib that was unfortunately steamrolled by the pre-recorded voices of the animals. Pre-recorded voices are terrible improvisers, by the way. Stump was stuck, unable to get herself back on her feet... or roots, I suppose. There was nothing to be done but be dragged off stage, in full view of the audience, by disgruntled Stage Hand Bob in a sweaty, stained Guess Who t-shirt from the 70's. Stump emerged from her stump that night in abject misery; what could she possibly do with her career now? Who could want a performer that couldn't even portray an inanimate object without falling over?

It took a few treks across our great continent, but you'll be happy to know that Stump-after-stump has pulled a full recovery. She's back to her routine of finding random strangers in Austin or Halifax or Saskatoon to party with. Stump has gone on to happy times in many other more gratifying roles within the company. The one benefit of playing Stump is that any role you take after that feels like King Lear.

As economic factors continue to encourage low-tech over high-tech solutions, other Stump-roles have been created within this company. There was Snail in *The Turtle Show*. Snail felt so guilty about not exercising enough during shows that she refused to eat the catering. You'd find her, a gaunt and desiccated husk, eating cat-food out of a can in the ladies dressing room.

I also once took on a stump role in *The Show About the Rat*. I was placed under a couch for the entire first act, my sole duty to manipulate an inflatable dragon by pushing it when it talked during a single song that had absolutely nothing to do with the rest of the show. That tour was a constant fight against the dark forces of Stumpdom. I thought the best thing to do was to keep my mind occupied while I waited under the sofa. I got an ebook reader and tried my best to keep myself distracted. But still my mind grew more Stumpish everyday. It wasn't until late in the tour—on a day I accidentally forgot my reader in the dressing room—that I realized an important truth. The only way to be happy while performing a task that is boring and pointless and repetitive is to give in to the banality and utterly commit yourself to that Sisyphean chore.

That day I plugged in the air compressor that inflated the dragon and gleefully pushed and shoved them with a deranged abandon that can only be described as psychotic. And it felt good.

After all if you're going to go crazy, it's better to be crazy happy than crazy sad.

THE DAY THE FAN STOOD STILL

Life on the road can be a little disorienting. Everything you were worried about back home is temporarily suspended. Haven't been to the dentist in two years? Haven't filed your taxes in three? Wanted by the police for a series of public nudity charges? Head out onto the road and put it all on hold for two or three months!

When you're out there on the road your only responsibility is to be in the hotel lobby at the appointed call. From there you get in a van and tune out. If you're hungry, just grab a sandwich from the place you've stopped for gas. Or a bag of Doritos and a two litre bottle of Diet Coke. Or a Red Bull and a pack of cigarettes. You know, whatever floats your boat.

You arrive at the theatre, drop your bag off in the dressing room and go to the green room to look at pictures of cats on the internet until you're called to the stage to check the spacing on what is inevitably going to be a stage that's too shallow or too narrow or not a stage at all, just a bunch of risers loosely stacked on top of each other in an arena. Once you're done, back to the internet cats until catering arrives. After the show it's back to the hotel to repeat it all the next day.

But the human mind does not appear to be designed to adjust well to such a responsibility-free existence. Inevitably it will invent some bullshit upon which it dwells until it drives itself absolutely turd-flinging crazy.

One day, a few weeks into my tour, the fan in my Head broke. This small, underpowered fan was the only thing, so I believed, that kept me from dying of heat stroke in that bear costume. It sucked precious fresh air into the head for me to breathe and prevented my hair from bursting into flames. It was an absolutely necessary part of my survival, and I didn't notice that it broke until near the end of the show.

Though in all likelihood the fan had been not been operating for the entirety of the second act, I started panicking. I could feel the sweat collecting on my scalp. The air felt close, with a dwindling percentage of oxygen in each lungful. By the time the curtain fell I ripped the head off, gasping for air. I ran into the wings, to notify our technician of this catastrophe.

She looked at me with deadened, exhausted eyes and told me she'd look into it after they got the set packed into the truck. I went back to the hotel where I got drunk on rye from the liquor store and ginger ale from the vending machine, regaling my colleagues with the tale of my broken fan, and how it was the worst thing that had ever happened to me ever in a million zillion years and that I almost died and it was the worst. And they agreed that broken fans were the worst. Ever.

The next day we went through the same hotel/van/gas station/van/theatre/greenroom-with-cats-on-the-internet routine. The houselights went down, the music started pumping and I put on my Head. But wait! Where was that familiar hum that promised fresh air and comfort? The fan was still broken! I ripped the head off and ran to the technician who was busy sewing a costume needed in the second act that had been damaged in transit somehow.

"My fan! My fan!" I cried out, "You didn't fix it!"

"I put new batteries in last night," she said without looking up from her work.

"It doesn't need batteries, it's broken!"

"I'll look at it during intermission."

Intermission! That meant I had to endure an entire hour (well, closer to 45 minutes) of utter agony! This was the worst! The worst ever! EVER!

Brave soul that I am, I admitted there was nothing to be done but go forth and do the best I could given the circumstances. I went out there and gave an entirely lackluster performance, for which I congratulated myself for surviving, knowing I had bravely taken one for the team.

But after intermission the fan still refused to budge. The technician informed me that a wire was loose and needed to be soldered back into place. She could fix it, but not until the next day. I would just have to make do.

Make do! This was an outrage! Did she not know how I suffered? Did she not know that this was the worst ever!? Ever in a million zillion years!!

I plodded through the second act, desperate to preserve enough energy to make it through without dying from dehydration, or suffocation, or spontaneous combustion. I slammed the head down on the prop table and stormed out to the van where I was driven back to the hotel to get drunk with bottles of gin and ginger ale, where I again related to the sympathetic audience of my cast-mates how the company was lucky that I was such a consummate professional. And they agreed that the company was lucky and that broken fans were the worst ever.

As a great deal of distance needed to be covered the following day, the company decided to fly the cast to our next destination instead of taking the van. We needed to be well rested after all. The crew, meanwhile, drove the van and truck over night across the Rockies in mid-February.

Our flight was the worst ever, by the way.

We landed in Calgary and had lots of time for naps and internet cat pictures before the truck arrived, eight hours behind schedule as they were stuck on a snowed-out mountain road for the entire night. They madly scrambled to get the set unloaded from the truck and set up on time for the show that evening.

Unwilling to leave anything to chance I found our beleaguered technician madly distributing props from their cases to the respective sides backstage. I enquired about my fan, and she assured me, she would get to it. I was not confident.

Nevertheless while we were eating our catering in the greenroom, there she was; sandwich in one hand, soldering gun in the other, fixing my fan.

When I immersed myself in the Head I could hear the hum that I'd been missing for the last few days. I marched on stage emboldened by the knowledge that I would be performing cool and refreshed and with plenty of good old O2!

But something happened by the middle of the first act. I was hot as balls again. I was certain my fan must have shorted out again, but when I listened, I could hear it going. It was then that I actually thought back to every show I'd done up until the point my fan broke and realized that I was always short of breath and always sweating like a water balloon made of burlap. The fan helped… but only a little.

And I'd made my exhausted, stressed out technician fix it while she ate a sandwich. No one should have to solder fans into bear heads while eating sandwiches. Sandwich-eating time should be sacred. But she did it without complaining, because it needed to get done.

I had lost perspective and, like a dead star, started sucking everything else in the Universe into my crazy. I felt so bad about the sandwich/soldering that I helped the crew load the set into the truck for a couple shows until they asked me to stop getting in their way. Hooray for being useless! Hooray for being an actor!

BEAR'S GUIDE TO HOTEL COOKERY

The table is set. The candles are lit. The wine is decanted. It's time for a romantic dinner at home.

And by home I mean hotel room. And by table I mean the double bed we eat on, not the double bed we sleep on. And by candles I mean florescent lights. And by decanted wine, I mean wine drunk directly from the bottle.

But it's still romantic in it's own do-it-yourself kind of way. It takes a lot of effort to create delicious meals with ingredients combined from what you found at a local grocery store, what you stole from catering, and the stale sort-of-food that have been sitting in the hotel vending machines for the past ten years.

By the way, corn chips do not improve with age.

There are many reasons why you might go through the difficult task of cooking in your hotel room. You might be a dancer who fears being unable to exercise restraint while repeatedly visiting American restaurants where the weekly caloric intake of an entire African village is considered a reasonable portion for a single meal. Or you might be of the cheap persuasion—after a lifetime of belt-tightening in a less than wealthy family you become unwilling to shell out that much money for dinner and tip every night, despite the fact that you are given per diem for that express purpose. You are obsessed with saving money, and damn it all, you will bank that per diem.

I once spent eight months singing on a cruise ship. While there I was unable to do any meal preparation myself—we were prohibited from bringing food (which could lead to rat/insect infestations), and any kitchen appliances (which could lead to fire) into our cabins. Though my privileged status as entertainer meant I didn't have to endure what passed for food in the crew mess (fish heads, anyone?), I was still restricted to eating food that was prepared by someone else, delivered to my seat. Sounds like luxury, but meal preparation was one of the things I missed most about normal life.

There's a profound banality to the act of routine cooking. And when you spend each night in a different hotel room, different city, or different country there can be a great deal of comfort in that kind of pedestrian activity. The hotel room becomes a surrogate home through the act of cooking in it.

But how do you maintain any quality of life when your hotel rooms only occasionally have a mini-fridge or microwave?

There needs to be a certain amount of preparation before you set out on the road to ensure you have the necessary supplies. Much of this stuff is available from dollar stores or the camping section of sporting goods retailers. Exactly what you need will depend on what kinds of foods you want to eat. Failure to prepare will result in the consumption of easy-open cans of cat food. This is not recommended. Unless you are a cat.

-Paring knife (with a plastic cover to prevent accidental stabbings while hauling your bag around)

-Can opener

-Fork or Spork or Knifsporkpatuladle

-Cutting board (as a courtesy to hotels who probably don't want you butchering chickens on their end tables)

-resealable spice containers (or it's going to be a bland tour)

-Small George Foreman Grill. (Grills endorsed by other boxers are also acceptable, with the notable exception of Mike Tyson's Grill, which is designed solely for grilling human ears)

-A fabric freezer bag

-Dish soap (in a well sealed container unless you want to smell like lemons)

-Some combination of all of these contained in a single tool labelled with Switzerland's flag

A hotplate can be a good idea, but then you need a pot and now you're talking about a whole lot of extra weight that you have to haul in and out of your room every day. I have travelled with actors who pack a full kitchen into their bag, complete with a sous chef and an industrial bread kneader. This is a decision you need to make after careful consultation with your spine and musculoskeletal system.

While not all hotels have a microwave, almost all have a coffee maker, which can be valuable tool for heating up soups. You can also do a pretty decent poached salmon filet. Just don't use it to try to make Stove Top stuffing. That experiment was a surprisingly disgusting failure.

While not all hotels have bar fridges, almost all have ice-machines and sinks—fill a plastic bag with ice, put it in the sink and you've got yourself what me and the missus like to call a *sinkfridge*. It probably wouldn't pass health code, but we're trying to save up to buy a condo, dammit!

Find the nearest grocery store, raid your venue's catering and conduct some experiments. With these tools, and a little ingenuity, you can open up a world of culinary delights. And by world of culinary delights, I mean a whole lot of salads.

REMEMBERING BIRD

Montpellier, France. Three years ago.

The cast was scattered around the breakfast room in our hotel as beams from the rising sun cut hard shadows across the room. The morning people were chatting with each other. Everyone else was drinking espresso and staring at their plates of cheese and bread—wishing they were extra large drip coffees and bacon and eggs. My wife and I were packing sandwiches for later. In ten minutes we would pile into vans and drive to the theatre where we were rehearsing for the first leg of our European tour.

One cast member was missing. Bird. But no one really expected Bird to be on time, anywhere, ever. He just showed up in his own time and in his own way. Sometimes you would arrive at breakfast and he'd have been there for two hours already, prying dark secrets out of the concierge with whom he was now best friends. Sometimes he'd explode into the room seconds before we were to leave, stuffing fistfuls of pastry and cheese into his jacket pocket before dashing out the door.

That morning we found him outside, still dressed in his

clothes from the previous day, reeking of cigarettes and booze, drinking the biggest cup of coffee he could find in France—which would hardly have passed for a medium in North America.

The previous afternoon, Bird decided to explore the city on foot. Without a map. He got himself good and lost, but was determined to find his way back to the hotel on foot—which he accomplished sixteen hours later, moments before we were to depart for the theatre for rehearsal.

In Paris, the city of taking yourself way too seriously to celebrate Halloween, Bird spent days building an elaborate vending machine costume out of tape, markers, and cardboard he dove into our hotel's dumpster to retrieve. Inside his cardboard monstrosity he'd built a chute that he would pour candy down to a crotch level dispenser slot if you gave him a kiss. He wandered the streets of Paris, chanting "Machine à bisous!", distributing candy to and receiving kisses from everyone he passed.

Also in Paris, Bird decided it would be fun to take a picture of himself in each Metro station—but do it in alphabetical order. He hadn't even finished the C stations before the subway shut down for the night. He would have finished the job too—if we hadn't packed up to drive to Geneva the next day.

I'll admit that there were times on that tour that due to exhaustion, or boredom, or whatever was bugging me that day, I gave less than stellar performances. But not Bird. It didn't matter how hung-over he was, or how little sleep he'd gotten, or how bad his legs hurt after wandering aimlessly from one end of a city to the next, every moment he was on stage was a hundred percent committed. Every second of his life was a hundred percent committed.

And that was how Bird lived off stage too. Every week he needed to ask the road manager for an advance on his per diem because he'd already spent it all buying rounds of drinks for total strangers in disreputable bars in reputable towns. Or on construction materials for outlandishly elaborate costumes. Or on American style extra-large coffees – which cost about one thousand Euros each.

One year later I saw Bird walking past my condo building. As my unit is on the second floor(with a spectacular view of a Japanese restaurant) I shouted down to him to wait. I met him at one of the seven Starbucks within a two block radius of my condo and bought him a coffee, despite his protestations that he treat me.

He looked like he'd been hit by a bus. He was skinny and sallow and his hair was thin. But he was the same Bird, through and through. Still telling me about how he was bouncing around sublets until the next month when he planned to spend some time with his family in Ottawa while he got chemotherapy.

Wait, what?

It turns out he hadn't been hit by a bus. He'd been hit by cancer. And as he told me it was working it's way through his system and that his prospects weren't good he did it with a kind of rushed disinterest. He was much more curious to know how me and the missus were doing, and what projects we were working on, and how we were enjoying living in our condo we'd bought after saving up by eating in our hotel rooms.

As far as he was concerned, his battle with cancer was one of the least interesting of his myriad of whacky adventures he was in the midst of. And he would much rather gleefully tell us about how he'd tricked this artist friend of his into drawing a picture of a cartoon character he'd dreamed up who looked like a tall brown tree log called "Paduce" after demanding that his friend "draw Paduce, draw Paduce, draw Paduce!" (or "Drop a deuce" or in layman's terms, "take a shit")

A few months after this chance encounter outside my condo, bird was dead. He knew, even then while we talked, that he had only a few months to live. But up to that point he'd always lived as though each day were his last. Why should he suddenly change now that that was literally the case?

After his very sudden death, we all struggled to glean some kind of meaning from his extraordinary life. Some interpreted it as a call to live life to the fullest—look at how rich his life was in experiences, look at how many lives he touched. We should all be like Bird, they said.

But for most of us, life is chaotic and difficult enough without actively looking for trouble. Bird did not have a retirement plan, and Bird probably couldn't have ever held down an office job. He would have continued living from one wacky misadventure to the next. Most of us are not cut out to be Birds. But we should be so lucky to as to have a Bird or two in our lives to take us on their exploits with them.

THAT WHICH CANNOT BE NAMED

Last night my wife and I were enjoying a game of *You Don't Know Jack* when one of the questions featured two words that sent her into an immediate panic. This state of inconsolable, albeit brief, terror at the mere mention of these words, a full year after the original incident, may point to the development of post-traumatic stress disorder.[2] What were these words that can reliably trigger this terrified response?

Bed. Bugs.

After spending several months each year living from hotel to hotel it becomes a question of when, not if, you will encounter these shitheads.[3] However, on this tour, my wife was lucky enough to encounter them not once, but twice. I was not on the tour in question when my partner's brain was wrecked by these blood-sucking assholes,[4] but I have had the pleasure of dealing with a now

---

2 My opinion as a qualified amateur pop-psychologist, well versed in a number of bullshit theories and self-help books.

3 I hope my conservative family will forgive my use of strong language, but bed bugs are honestly the shittiest shithead shitshits in the world. Shit.

4 See above footnote.

totally neurotic wife.

Typically on tour we stay at whatever hotel the show has a sponsorship deal with. On this tour there was no sponsorship deal, so the company booked the cast into hotels where they could get cheap deals. However, the cast didn't end up staying at these discount(read: obviously bed bug ridden) hotels because the road manager had previously worked on the North American Justin Bieber tour and had amazing connections to all the fanciest(read: probably should not have bed bugs) hotels.

So, thanks to a well connected road manager, the cast lived it up in hotels worthy of an adolescent multi-platinum pop star, completely free from concern that they might get infected from the brain-melting horror the scientific community calls Cimex lectularius.[5]

I will not name any of these TWO fancy hotels where my wife found bed bugs. I'm not particularly keen to open myself up to libel charges. However, both hotels, hotels fancy enough that they had been graced by the presence of the Biebs himself, had bed bugs in the bedding.

Who knows? Maybe Justin Bieber is responsible for the recent surge in bed bug activity... I hadn't really heard of them as a problem until he burst onto the scene. Maybe he caused the outbreak!

My God... Maybe he IS a bed bug himself!?[6]

Both hotels subjected her bags and clothes to steaming. They assured her that she would be fine, and that this never, ever, not in a million years, happens in their hotels.

When she returned home to Toronto, I was only with her for a week before I flew out of town for a Christmas gig in Saskatchewan. Shortly after I left, she made the alarming discovery

---

5 Or Lifewrecking Demonshits because even the scientific community thinks they're the worst.

6 You read it here first, folks. Justin Bieber is, at the very least, at the centre of a global bed bug conspiracy.

that the hotels hadn't successfully steamed all the eggs out of her bags—and that the jerks had hatched and were having a gay old time taking over our home.

She immediately called me and I threw everything I had with me out into what is supposed to be the ungodly cold of a Canadian prairie winter. Temperatures of – 30°C are not uncommon at this time of year in Saskatchewan. I would know—I grew up in that frozen wasteland. A bed bug will only last about 15 seconds in – 30°C temperatures. Even at – 15°C they'll only last a few days. However this particular year, for whatever reason, God decided that he would bless the prairies with the mildest winter I'd ever experienced. It was only two weeks later that the temperature got cold enough that any contaminant that may have made its way into my bags would have died the horrible freezing death that it deserved.

My wife was completely traumatized by the experience. She felt violated and ashamed and dirty. She did everything she could have to prevent them from spreading—after each incident she threw out her luggage and most of her clothes. She couldn't enjoy the company of friends—she constantly worried about contaminating others.

I'm happy to say that we've been living bed bug free for a year now. However, I can no longer eat anything in bed. Any dropped crumb can and will be mistaken for a bed bug. Any blemish on my pasty white skin will be immediately interpreted as a bed bug bite, rather than what it usually is… bacne. Bed bugs have become that which cannot be named. Their mere mention, say by a humorous trivia game, causes hours of anxiety.

Jusin Bieber, this is your fault. I demand an apology.

CAPTAIN UNICYCLE'S BLOG

Captain Unicycle was a clown. Like an actual clown that went to clown school and did specialized clown workouts in hotel fitness centers. He spent his summers touring his very successful solo clown/juggling/unicycle act to street festivals around the world. But in the winter, without street festivals to go to, he had to take work where he could get it. And this meant touring with us.

Which he hated—a lot.

Captain Unicycle was used to moving according to his own schedule. He hated waiting in the lobby for everyone to gather before heading to the theatre. He hated waiting in the greenroom for everyone to get packed up after the show. He especially hated sitting in the van with the rest of the cast as we were driven from town to town.

Captain Unicycle even hated performing in the shows, which required him to adhere to a rigid script. His Captain Unicycle solo act lived and died by absolute spontaneity. He hated that the only clown skill he learned from clown school and practised in his clown workouts was riding his unicycle.

But more than anything else he hated that he had to sing. Oh, how he hated to sing.

This adds up to a whole lot of hate. But for a while Captain Unicycle did his best to remain pleasant with the rest of the cast. Everyone knew he was unhappy, but as a lot of unhappy people escape real life by going on the road, that was nothing remarkable. Eventually he couldn't take it any more and quit. But while he was there, trapped with a bunch of people who annoyed the hell out of him, moving according to a schedule that annoyed the hell out of him, and doing a show that annoyed the hell out of him, he discovered an outlet to let all that pent up aggression out: blogging!

Captain Unicycle loved his blog. His blog filled that void in his soul. In his blog he could finally express all his frustration at the banality of the show or the stupidity of his cast-mates.

But Captain Unicycle found himself in a quandary. He loved everything about his blog—except the fact that no one read it. Page counts were low. No subscribers. No comments. And he couldn't stand that something he was so proud of should go unread.

To help drum up readers, Captain Unicycle insisted that his castmates, the very fodder for his daily polemics, read his latest blog posts. But Captain Unicycle wasn't stupid. He didn't want to piss everyone off and spend the rest of his tour alienated from the cast. So he masked their identities behind pseudonyms so nobody would know who he was writing about. Kind of like I'm doing by calling him Captain Unicycle.

I'm not sure what was going through Captain Unicycle's mind that made him think this was a good idea. The earnest way he encouraged people to read his blog, and the compliment fishing that would go on after someone had, suggest that he really seemed to believe that his use of pseudonyms would prevent people from recognizing themselves despite his detailed and unflattering physical descriptions of them, and the insulting re-telling of specific events they had been involved in mere hours before the publication of the post.

I thought for a while that he was deliberately being a shit-disturber. But then he'd come down and join us at the hotel bar as though he hadn't just insulted every person sitting around the table with him. He sincerely seemed like he wanted the companionship. But all those he'd insulted in his blog thus far would either ignore him, or be outright hostile.

Captain Unicycle would get upset at being ostracized by the cast. And he would express his frustrations in his blog. Lather, rinse, repeat.

He was torn between the needs of Captain Unicycle the human being and Captain Unicycle the artist. Captain Unicycle the human being needed friends. Captain Unicycle the artist needed validation. And what Captain Unicycle ended up doing was to value the people he worked with more as potential readers than as potential friends.

Captain Unicycle no longer tours with children's theatre. He still tours his solo-act to street festivals. I would highly recommend his act—but at the end make sure you toss some money into the hat. Otherwise, you might end up on his blog.

DO YOU KNOW WHO I AM?

Occasionally companies hire us to bring some of the popular characters from our shows to do guest appearances and meet-and-greets at events like street festivals, exhibitions, or ceremonial Christmas tree lightings. It can get pretty unpleasant, particularly at outdoor events in the summer.

At least the pay is good.

I rarely do the big meet-and-greets in costume. I get really anxious knowing I'm surrounded by thousands of children and not able to outrun them if it came to that. More often, I help out as a wrangler—guiding the costumed characters around and fielding questions for them. But even that has its share of annoyances.

The wrangler is the one who needs to keep the line from descending into a chaotic man-in-the-state-of-nature Hobbesian nightmare. You've got to deal with the parents who blatantly cut in front of hundreds of other families in line and then feign the inability to speak English when you ask them to line up like a decent human being. Usually the best way to deal with them is just to let them get their picture, get rid of them, and apologize to the next family in line. If you can get their photo in fast enough, then hurry the next kid into picture-taking position, the parents get too distracted trying to prepare for the shot to realize how outraged they are.

A wrangler's most important job is protecting the poor souls inside the costumes. I don't know enough about child psychology to understand why, after seeing their favourite cartoon bear, one would immediately launch into the kind of full frontal assault that would impress a regiment of late medieval heavy cavalry. But it happens, usually to the humiliation of the parents involved.

One such assault occurred at a season opening party for a team in the Canadian Football League. There were four or five characters total and I was assigned as the guardian of Penguin. The event was moving along well until one blonde, five-year-old treasure decided it would be super fun to punch Penguin in the stomach as hard as he could. I stepped between him and the injured Antarctic bird and said, "Whoa, take it easy there, little buddy! Not so rough, okay?"

Usually after such displays of gratuitous childhood violence, a very embarrassed parent rushes in, apologizes, and then drags their sociopathic rage machine away. But this time there was no parent. Just a very tired looking Filipino woman who silently toted him off.

I asked Penguin if she was okay. She gave me the thumbs up and we continued moving through the line up. But that was not the last we were to see of our blonde-haired little treasure.

I don't know what he had against Penguin, but he returned a second time. This time he accosted Penguin while I was trying to teach a grown man how to use his own camera. By the time I was able to step between them, Blondie got in another punch in the stomach and a kick in the shins. Penguin shoved God's gift to humanity away and I stepped between them saying, "Calm down, little guy! Where's your mom and dad?"

The angelic little cutie pie spit on the ground and disappeared into the throng of families, pursued by his flagging Filipino supervisor. Penguin assured me she was okay and we worked through the remaining families as quickly as possible to avoid any further assaults. I walked the animals back to the change room, then got to work packing up to go home.

It was here I was approached by an enraged, spray-tan orange, blonde haired monstrosity.

"How dare you tell my son to calm down!"

It would have taken a blind and deaf person in a vegetative coma to have been unable to draw the connection between son and mother. I've dealt with a lot of crappy, aggressive kids in my day, and a lot of crappier, more aggressive parents. But even the worst parents usually turn into puddles of contrition after their darling little demons blatantly assault someone in a mascot costume. People realize there are lines you don't cross. The person in that suit is suffering enough as it is.

But this woman didn't seem to get it.

"How dare you tell my son to take it easy! He is a good boy!" she continued.

I really didn't know what to say in response. The gears were working in my head, but the only logical response I could come up with was that it was my responsibility to the rest of humanity to throw this woman off a cliff. I still believe that would have probably been the best thing to have done, from a long-term, strictly Utilitarian point of view. But some selfish part of me knew that if I threw her off a cliff I would wind up in jail, so I failed to do my duty to humanity. And for that I am sorry.

I was so utterly dumbfounded the only thing I could think to say was:

"What?"

"He's just a little rambunctious and that Penguin had no right to shove him!"

I still had no response whatsoever. So my previous one seemed like it would suffice.

"What?"

"Do you know who I am?" the orange woman demanded.

"A very tall Oompa Loompa?" Is what I did not say. What I did say was:

"What?"

"Do you know who I am?"

"What?"

"My husband is the owner of this team."

"What?"

"I could have you fired!"

"What?"

It was at this point that she stormed off, never to be heard from again. It could be that she told her long suffering husband about the ordeal and he just rolled his eyes, and once again calculated how much fifty percent of his property added up to. Or it could be that I had simply called her bluff and she stormed off to drink sour apple martinis or flavourless, low-carb, low-calorie beer with the other VIP moms. Who knows? All I know is that I wasn't fired or even reprimanded.

I drove home that night and thought about how I could have handled the encounter better. I kept thinking of other clever one-liners with which I could have zinged her, but knew that would have only escalated the problem. I could have apologized and tried to calm her down, but I doubt that would have helped. All I did was wait out the storm, and, to be honest, I think that was probably the best thing.

After all, if we seriously answer the question "Do you know who I am?" the answer paints a relatively sympathetic picture. I do know who she is. She is the fading token wife of a wealthy sports team owner. Nobody wants to be that.

I don't resent the kid for being a maniac. Some kids are just crazy. They have more energy than they know what to do with, and no sense of how to channel it yet. I was one of those maniacs.

But my parents knew I could be difficult to deal with. They apologized to my teachers when I decided to answer all questions in song or creatively re-interpreted my homework assignments in some smart-ass way. I would feel terrible for what my parents had to go through, except that I know that, Karmaically, I will eventually have some screaming, puking maniac of my own to apologize for.

The problem isn't the shitty kids. The problem is the shitty parents who do nothing but drink sour apple martinis and take pictures on their iPads while exasperated Filipino nannies chase down their darling little demons.

BUY THE MERCH

I recently performed in a British style Pantomime over the holidays. At our closing night party the producer and I got into a discussion during which he bemoaned how little money he'd made in the end, despite the fact that tickets to the show nearly sold out and their merchandise (tiaras and fairy wands) was cleaned out half-way through the run. Digging a little deeper, I asked about pricing for their merchandise and discovered the key to his poor revenue.

When I toured as Bear with The Children's Theatre Company they raked money in hand over fist—particularly from the merch. I recall a particularly lucrative three show stint in Calgary following which our road manager threw the seventy thousand dollars worth of merch proceeds onto his hotel room bed to roll around in.

The Children's Theatre Company sets up their merch table in such a way that once you enter the lobby, no matter where your seats are in the auditorium you must pass by it. Once the child scans the table and sees the light-up wands, something snaps inside their brains. They must have it. And if it means crying so hard they actually crap themselves, so help them God, they will fill their pants.

Many more stubborn parents rush past the merch table and ignore their darling angel's pleas for a light-up wand. They hurry to their seats, hoping that by the time they get into the darkened auditorium their child will have forgotten about he wants.

Wrong. So wrong.

The brilliant thing about selling light-up wands is that in a darkened auditorium they are self-marketing. The child will be surrounded by hundreds of other kids waving around the cheap, plastic pieces of garbage. The child will escalate the conflict as far as it needs to go to get their own wand.

The question that the Children's Theatre Company asks themselves is not what is a fair price to charge for this light up wand, but, and this is important, *how much is a parent willing to pay to make their kid shut up?* For many exhausted and stressed out parents, ten or fifteen dollars is nothing if it brings them a bit of peace. A child will always win a war of attrition.

Movie theatres understand that pricing is dependent on what people are willing to pay—that's why you have to refinance your house to get a popcorn and soda. Once you're in the lobby and you smell that sickly sweet aroma (that is somehow appealing despite the fact that it actually smells like urine mixed with butter and sugar) you can't help yourself. You would be willing to open a vein and pour out a litre of blood if that's what they asked. You would beat another man to death with your bare fists and wear his skin as a cape. You would leave your firstborn child to be ground up for hotdog meat. Yet all they ask is $11.50 for a large popcorn and soda combo that probably cost them a total of thirty cents for the actual materials and even less for the minimum wage they pay the sweaty teenager who sold it to you? What a deal!

The producer of the pantomime did not understand this principle. He bought his wands and tiaras from a dollar store for a buck-fifty each. He didn't want to seem greedy, so he sold them for five bucks a piece. Now you might say to yourself that 333% price margin is still pretty good. But by buying directly from a supplier and charging what the market would bear, The Children's Theatre Company can yield a much tastier margin of 1333%.

I once took a friend and her five-year-old daughter to a show my wife was touring and was able to see for myself the whole thing play out. There was one particularly adorable moment when one of the characters on stage asked the kids in the audience to shout out a wish they had. My friend's daughter pointed to the kid next to her and screamed, "I WISH FOR ONE OF THOSE WANDS!"

A very clever mother a few seats down was obviously no rookie when it came to coming to see children's theatre. The second they got to their seats she pulled a dollar store light up wand of her own out of her purse for each of her children.

Your vision is pretty bad inside one of those mascot heads. The small hole you see through is covered with black mesh so no one can see the self-hating person inside. There have been times that the amount of light-up wands sold probably saved my life. The time I fell off the stage was before our merch truck had arrived. And there were a few near misses after we sold out. When everything is black it can get hard to distinguish where the wings end and the edge of the stage begins. When you have hundreds—sometimes thousands—of children waving glowing wands, it becomes very clear which direction you do not want to go.

All of this to say that, though it's expensive, for the sake of the poor, nearly blind bastards in the bear suits, buy your kid a wand.

FART PROTOCOL

My wife's been complaining a lot these days about how the cast on her current tour seems completely incapable of controlling their flatulence. This came as a great shock to me, as there are few people in the world who enjoy a nice fart as much as my missus. She once bragged that she let out such a loud rumbler that it awoke her sleeping roommate. I was quick to point out the irony that she, of all people, should complain about people expressing their gassy selves.

She assured me that the situation had moved beyond all reasonable measures. She's had to introduce a number of what she calls "Fart Protocols" to keep the situation from spiralling out of control.

The first thing she did was ban certain items from the rider. The company allots forty dollars per show that the tour manager can use to buy snacks for the cast before shows. What the rider includes isn't set in stone. Depending on how flexible/awesome the tour manager is, you can graze on the rider food for lunch and dinner without dipping into your per diem. Typically the rider will include a veggie tray, some pita and hummus, some sports drinks or juice, cookies, crackers or some cheese.

Hummus was the first thing to be banned from the rider. No one digests chickpeas very well. It's pure fart fuel.

Dairy was the next to go. Some nutritionists argue that the consumption of dairy into adulthood is unnatural. After being trapped in a van with a bunch of people who just ate cheese, yogurt, and ice cream on a drive from New York to North Tonawanda, I'm inclined to think you'd agree. If the UN ever finds out what happened in that van, everyone will be tried as a war criminal for the production of biological weapons.

One girl claimed that all the aspartame from diet drinks was the reason for her obscene methane production. So aspartame was the next to go, whether there was any validity to the assertion or not.

New in-van rules have been created. In warmer climates, windows can be left open, keeping the air in the van circulating. In Northern Ontario in February, you do not have this luxury. Once someone befouls the van air by breaking wind, all windows are opened and everyone is given thirty seconds to clear out whatever gas they've currently got built up. At the conclusion of the gas-expulsion-period the windows are rolled up again, and the occupants are encouraged to try to contain themselves until the van at least warms up again. This is called the Fart Festival, Fart Symphony, or the Fartchestra.

Maybe it's working in children's entertainment that causes people's sense of humor to degenerate to one that exclusively revolves around farting. One girl—who played the character Owl —would shout a count down from inside her animal head. From inside my own head I could hear the muffled shout "THREE, TWO, ONE!" Then she'd let out a trumpet style fart—the kind that you really have to push to get out. Thank God she never had diarrhoea. Everyone likes the smell of their own brand, but when you fart in one of those mascot costumes, you severely Dutch Oven yourself. The only escape is to get the air circulating in the head by running around really fast.

I've been on some tours where we've experienced some pretty hilarious/tragic flatulence problems, but I've never experienced anything as endemic as what my wife describes to me over the phone. I thought about it for a while, and I think I've isolated why this cast is so much fartier than any other cast either of us have worked with.

I think it's actually a pretty smart idea, so I'm going to coin a term that I really hope catches on. I call it Falk's Law. Please use that expression as often as you can—I'd like to be famous for something, and it might as well be fart theory. Anyway, here it is.

FALK'S LAW

The further a balance of genders in any group of people moves to either extreme, the higher the chances said group will devolve into a toxic fart factory.

The tour my wife is currently on features an almost exclusively female cast—and yes, for those of you who still cling to outdated notions of the fairer sex, women's digestive systems operate in the exact same way as men's. There's something about not needing to worry about grossing out potential sexual partners that allows people to really let loose. And when I say "let loose" I mean it in the most literal interpretation of that expression possible. Even if everyone in the van has husbands or wives or boyfriends or girlfriends back home, social stigma tied to base evolutionary impulses keeps a lid on any gaseous excesses.

I haven't fully field tested my theory, so I don't know how it would work in all circumstances. For example what about a van full of women and homosexual men? It is my hope that further research will be conducted by some enterprising doctoral students that will prove and refine the theory.

In the meantime, if you make plans to go on a road trip with a group of friends, consider inviting along some members of the opposite sex to help keep the air free of anal pollutants.

DUMPSTER DIVING IN MARSEILLE

Two months into our three month tour of French-speaking Europe, Turtle stepped out of the Marseille subway station near our theatre to discover her wallet had gone missing.

That day, groups of us had separated to explore the town until we had to be back at the theatre for our show in the evening. I don't remember what everyone else had gotten up to that day. Me and the missus went around exploring local landmarks and feigning interest in buying a Nespresso machine in order to get free coffee.

A member of our French crew had made a special point of warning people to keep a close watch on their bags—pickpocketing was a major problem in Marseille. Having been warned, we all went about our adventures, sort of keeping an eye on our bags and pockets. But here's the thing about professional pickpockets: they're really really really good at it.

By the time me and the missus arrived back at the subway near our theatre, a group of my castmates had already gathered to try to figure out at what point the Turtle's wallet could have gone missing. Turtle had used her wallet to buy metro tickets—so she had it when she got on the subway. There didn't seem anything conspicuous about the ride itself—they were no strangers nearby on the uncrowded subway.

As she was leaving the subway, a group of teenagers appeared nearby, exiting through the turnstiles at the exact same time. In front of Turtle, a girl got her purse snagged in the turnstile and jolted to a stop—Turtle bumped into her, and another girl bumped into Turtle from behind. The whole exchange was so banal and rapid and naturally played, that Turtle didn't think anything of it. The girls didn't even apologize for bumping into her. In Canada an apology would be expected. In France it would be a dead giveaway that something was afoot. It wasn't until Turtle got above ground that she reached into her bag and discovered her wallet was no longer there.

Groups of us scoured the trashcans around the subway, hopeful that the pickpocketers would have just taken the cash and dumped the rest of the wallet, which unfortunately included Turtle's passport and any other form of identification she'd brought with her. The cash itself was a pretty devastating blow. That morning, we had just been given our 35 Euro per diem for the past two weeks. Those pickpocketers got away with 490 Euros—or close to $700 at the time. Losing your cash hurts financially—replacing your passport is time consuming, inconvenient, and hurts financially.

Our search of the nearby trashcans had failed to turn up any sign of her wallet, and we'd run out of time to search any further out. We were leaving Marseille immediately after the show, so we just had to resign ourselves that the wallet was gone for good. We got back to the theatre and reported the story to our road manager and set about getting ready for the show.

When we got our places call we put on our heads and got into positions in the wings. Turtle was devastated, but was taking it like a champ. There were a couple thousand kids out there who'd come to see her, so she had to leave her personal tragedy at the door. As the lights were dimming for the show, mere seconds before we were to run on stage to the screams of thousands of four to seven year olds, our road manager burst backstage waving the missing wallet in the air.

As soon as we left the production office to get suited up in our animal costumes, our road manager had set off on the Quixotic task of finding a single missing wallet in a city of 1.5 million people. We'd already searched all the trashcans in the immediate vicinity of the metro station. Our road manager expanded the search radius by a few blocks, which now included many trashcans on street corners and a number of large dumpsters in nearby alleys.

On his way back to the theatre, after a thoroughly unsuccessful search, he passed by a dumpster he'd already rummaged through previously. Something told him to take one final peek before giving up. He lifted the lid and poked in his head. His eye was caught by a mere centimetre of blue fabric poking out from underneath several bags of trash – way at the bottom of the nearly full dumpster. He climbed in, dug out the bags, and discovered the missing wallet, sans cash, but still containing the passport and other identification.

We all marvelled at the miraculousness of the find. What were the odds that he'd find it, in all the dumpsters in Marseille? What about the fact that he'd already searched that dumpster, but something told him to check again?

I don't want to steal God's thunder, but the fact is that the wallet wouldn't have been "miraculously" found if our road manager hadn't been willing to leap into dumpsters in a strange city to begin with. Miracles seem to be more frequent around people who are willing to get their hands dirty.

That day we were all stuck with the dilemma of taking our per diem with us and risking pickpocketers, or leaving it in the unsecured dressing rooms, where it could have just as easily been stolen. It could have been any of us who lost our money that day—

so we all pitched in twenty Euros to cover some of her loss.

Me and the missus took our per diem with us as well. But she insisted I wear one of those uncomfortable money belts that make it feel like you're wearing a diaper. I always resented having to wear that stupid thing. It made my crotch all sweaty. But after Marseille taught us that pickpocketing is a real thing that actually happens to real people I started shoving everything I could into that sweaty crotch pocket.

NINE HOURS OF TRIVIAL PURSUIT

Touring with *The Show About the Rat* was probably one of my most miserable professional experiences. The show was extremely popular which meant doing at least two shows a day in most cities, and the schedule was tightly packed. Show, show, drive, sleep. Show, show, drive, sleep. Show, show, drive, sleep. The booker who'd built the schedule counted days with only a four-hour drive as a day off. This person had obviously never had to sit in a van for at least four hours every day for twenty five days in a row.

The misery caused by this gruelling itinerary was compounded by personal problems many members of the cast were going through. Sheep had decided to go on this tour as an escape from the maelstrom of family and relationship issues that had been plaguing her for over a year. She could regularly be found crying in her dressing room. Or hotel room. Or the van. Or on stage.

Cat and Rat, a couple, had decided to go on a crazy person diet that required all meals to be eaten before 6 PM, and restricted them from eating any catering, restaurant food, and partaking in the lifeblood of any tour, alcohol. This meant that they had to travel with a suitcase filled with over 60 pounds of kitchen equipment and food, and that they couldn't go out to any bars or hotel room parties. Rat even refused to go out for Cat's birthday, so that he wouldn't have to face the temptation to break his diet. That's when you know your diet is a crazy person diet—when you refuse to go out for your girlfriend's birthday to keep at it.

Octopus had been experiencing a great deal of career success outside of touring children's theatre, and as such regretted accepting the tour to begin with.

Shooting Star was dancing on a foot injury that required surgery, and Dusteroo was still recovering from a severe back injury. The head of Rat's costume was designed too heavy and was causing him a great deal of neck pain. I sprained my shoulder trying to lift Cat and Rat's fully stocked kitchen/pantry/suitcase into the van.

I also started to develop the Stump Complex from my ridiculously simple and unrewarding role in the show, and so sought to fill my life with purpose through writing—which meant spending most free time by myself.

It all added up to a fragmented and isolated cast that grew increasingly miserable with each passing day. Even those with normally sunny dispositions were sullen and bitchy by day twenty five, which was when we finally got our first real day off.

There was one day, near the end of the our twenty five day marathon, that stands out in my memory as the one ray of sunshine from this tour, even though it was during a twelve hour drive day. It was the day of the nine-hour Trivial Pursuit marathon.

There are a lot of ways to kill time on a drive day. I always start each tour with the best intentions of using the time to get some writing or reading done. But once the van starts moving, all hopes of productivity get tossed aside. Looking at a page or word processor while driving across the mountains in the middle of winter is a recipe for instant pukesville. I can watch TV or movies on my laptop for a few hours as long as the roads aren't too bad. My wife can fall asleep pretty easily in the van, but I've never mastered the art of sleeping while cramped in a moving vehicle. I usually spend a lot of time listening to music and staring out the window until my nausea has abated enough to watch another episode of whatever show I'm power watching at the time.

I found the almost thirty-year-old edition of Trivial Pursuit at a used clothing store. I convinced a couple other people to play a heavily modified, board-less version of the game (that I called The Ultimate Trivial Pursuit Championship) while we drove from somewhere in the southern Canadian prairies up to somewhere in the Rocky Mountains.

We started the game with two teams—split up by rows in our fifteen passenger van. Each team was given a few minutes to answer all the questions on a single card, after which the other team could steal the questions for points. I didn't expect the game to last more than an hour, but eventually everyone joined the game (except Sheep who was too busy hating life) and the game went on and on and on.

We finally had to end the game after the tenth hour when it became too dark to read the cards. Everyone who participated was amazed at how quickly the day had passed.

From this point on, most of the cast seemed to make a more concerted effort to spend time together outside of when we were obliged to be together in the van or in the dressing room. I eased up on how much writing I was expecting myself to accomplish, and embraced how ridiculous my role in the show was. Cat eased up some of her dietary restrictions (though Rat maintained his diet and misery until the end of tour).

The irony is that when you start to feel like you need to get away from the people you work with, the problem may be that you aren't actually spending enough time together at all. You just have to choose to be together and invest emotionally in that time.

SHOOTING STAR IS DEAD INSIDE

I've come to realize that one of the biggest differences between a professional performer and an amateur performer is that the ability to perfectly conceal your contempt when working with less than stellar material.

Dusteroo had a very difficult time hiding his contempt for his role in *The Show About the Rat.*

Many of the people who work with the Touring Children's Theatre Company are relatively young theatre school grads who are looking for some cash and an opportunity to travel. And putting on a giant animal head that gives you headaches, or sweating your ass off in a costume that is essentially a full body rug, or sitting in a cramped van with someone who's eaten too much hummus is still better than slinging lattes at your neighbourhood Starbucks. Plus, you get to see some pretty cool places.

Unlike most his colleagues in their early to mid twenties, Dusteroo was decidedly on the wrong side of forty. A few years previous he'd quit his job and, with the support of his wife, pursued his dreams of becoming an actor. The Touring Children's Theatre

Company is great because most of its tours are through the fall to early spring—when it tends to be slower for film, TV, and other theatre.

So for Dusturoo, going on tour with a kid's show was a good way to make a few bucks doing something that was kind of like what he wanted to be doing, in a time when he probably wouldn't be making any money performing anyway.

He was getting sick of hiding behind the giant animal heads, as everyone inevitably does. But every show has a "host"—a character without an animal head who is able to improvise if something disastrous happens. Once while hosting, my wife had to play Simon Says with the audience for ten minutes while the crew madly fixed some technical problem. When you're talking about an audience of hundreds of children, you can't just turn on the house lights and announce that the play will resume in ten minutes without totally losing them.

So here's this forty-something guy, who didn't want to go out on the road anymore in a head character. But *The Show About the Rat* featured not one, but FIVE hosts. He jumped on the offer to play one of the host roles, in which he would portray a number of different characters (including the pseudonym I've been using for him, the Dusteroo). His face could be seen throughout and he would be mic'd for a live vocal. Real acting! What joy! What bliss!

But what killed the experience for poor old Dusteroo was his star costume, and the song and dance that went along with it.

The Shooting Star Song was one of the campiest, most painful things I've ever had to watch a grown heterosexual man perform eight to ten times a week. In it, Dusteroo was one of the backup singers/dancers to the "Shooting Star," and was dressed in a big, puffy, shiny, bright blue fabric star that had a little hole cut out in the topmost point for his face. His arms had to be outstretched at all times to keep the two side points from drooping. His spandex clad legs stuck out the middle of the bottom of the star. It was truly a hilarious costume, provided you weren't the poor bastard inside it.

In the twenty seven years since my first performance in a community theatre production of *The King and I* at the tender age of four, I have occasionally found myself involved in productions that I've known were not of the highest quality. As a teenager in a devout, church going family, I was constantly being roped into performing in the most ham-fisted "dramas" and the least funny "skits" the evangelical religious community could muster. In my professional career I have found myself cast in roles I was ill suited for (like when the twenty eight year old me was hired to play a fifteen year old skateboarder in a rock and roll musical—in which I actually had to skateboard[7]). I have thrice found myself engaged in professional revue shows that required me to rap—which means I've made considerably more money rapping than most people who actually consider themselves rappers ever will.[8]

Suffice it to say that, in the name of paying the bills, I've done some things on stage of which I've been less than proud.

I like to think that in all those circumstances I did my level best to conceal the contempt or embarrassment I felt. But to be honest, I don't think I have what it takes to be able to make the best of having to do the Shooting Star Song, and I hope to God I'm never put to the test.

The song was about "Shooting Star" trying to figure out what kind of "star" she should be. The accompanying choreography was upbeat and cute to the point of psychosis. Imagine Zooey Deschanel on crack, LSD, and a couple martinis after suffering

---

7 For anyone curious as to whether they should take up skateboarding in their late twenties, I cannot express in words how much of a bad idea this is.

8 For anyone curious as to the ethnic appropriateness of me rapping, consider that the reflected light from my naked torso in full daylight will cause your eyes to bleed. PS, why in God's name do people insist on putting rap songs into shows when they know damn well that the people who are going to end up performing it are white musical theatre nerds?

severe blunt head trauma. If the show weren't targeted to three to five year-olds, you'd wonder what kind of diseased mind could come up with this stuff. After an introduction in which Shooting Star wonders about all the different kinds of stars she could be (little stars, big stars, bright stars, etc…), she has this startlingly vapid revelation (and this is verbatim from the script):

"What kind of star shall I be tonight? Well it's simple! I will be who I am. And that's me! Because that's who I am!"

And then she launches into the song about being a "shooting" star.

The more you think about that line, the less sense it makes. It's the kind of thing that sounds like it's supposed to make sense, so you just let the sentiment wash over you. But when you really think about it, "I will be who I am. And that's me! Because that's who I am!" is absolutely meaningless. I'd say you can't write this crap, but the crazy thing is, someone actually did.

And there's poor old Dusteroo behind her, singing and dancing his little heart out, but utterly dead behind the eyes.

During rehearsals, Dusteroo asked me how a grown man was supposed to get through this song without feeling utterly humiliated. The only way I saw was to go deeper down the rabbit hole. Don't act as big as the women smiling and singing beside you. Go further. Smile bigger. Sing louder. Don't just grin and bear it. Don't just accept it. Don't even just embrace it. This is camp we're talking about. You've got to lube it up and shtup its brains out.

But Dusteroo couldn't. I don't think camp was in his vocabulary. He just put his star costume on every day and white-knuckled it until the song was over.

One of our technicians and I used to watch from the wings to try to fill in the inner monologue that must have been going through his head as he sang and danced the Shooting Star Song. What we came up with usually involved a lot of four letter words and repeated appeals to whatever higher power might be listening to put their smiting powers to full use.

After more than hundred shows spread out over two months, it never got any easier for Dusteroo. To this day, I think I could probably bring him to tears just by singing the Shooting Star Song in his presence.

THE DISAPPEARING RABBIT TRICK

While my motivation to tour had always been either the lure of a steady paycheck or fun destinations, there were those for whom the prime motivation to get out on the road was to escape the burdens of their normal life. Worries about booking a dental check-up, or filing your taxes, or returning that movie to Blockbuster which you haven't gotten around to in six years, are set aside for the weeks or months you're out on the road. After all, there's nothing you can do about them, so why worry? Just pop open a bottle of wine in the green room while you wait for the road manager to count up the merchandise proceeds before heading out to the next town. Before you know it, worries about dental health and tax obligations vanish along with the Blockbuster store itself.

But the problem with the kind of people who are running off to join the proverbial circus is that while they escape the stresses of actually dealing with their lives, they are introduced to a series of new stresses unique to that lifestyle. You sleep in a different bed each night. You spend every waking hour with the same eight to ten people. You spend months away from your significant other.

Though I've hung up my giant bear head for good, my wife still does quite a bit of touring. Of the last nine months, we've spent three and a half in the same city. I'm so used to sleeping alone that the last time she had a stop in Toronto, I quite nearly shat myself in panic when I got up in the middle of the night to take a piss and realized there was someone in my bed. After I screamed like a little girl, we had a good laugh about it at my expense. The subsequent realization about what it implied about our relationship was a little less hilarious.

One of the most obvious cases of a person who just needed to stop touring to deal with her life was Rabbit. She did about three tours too many, two of which I was on to witness her downward spiral.

We were booked to go on an epic tour of French-speaking Europe. People fought like crazy to get put on it. But the beginning of that tour was incredibly weird. Rabbit, along with two other women in the cast had ended long term relationships days before the tour was to depart. And on this tour, we spent close to a third of the nights sleeping in a big double decker tour bus, which meant that for the first couple weeks you could always hear at least one person sobbing inside their bunk over the hum of the bus's engine.

Rabbit was justifiably upset. A breakup with someone you believed you were going to be spending the rest of your life with is a pretty nasty shock. But, we all thought, here we are touring France, Belgium and Switzerland. Surely if anything could get her out of this funk, three months of gourmet food and fine wine should do the trick, despite all the cheese-induced-constipation.

But she was unrelentingly miserable. Some of the more dutiful members of the cast took turns taking her out with them as they explored some of the most beautiful cities in the world. Every day I grabbed my wife and we shot out of the tour bus like champagne corks. Me and the missus got married only weeks before the tour and I was not going to let anyone's negativity ruin our working honeymoon.

The next time I worked with Rabbit was over a year later. And that year had not been kind to her. An ill-conceived showmance[9] with a much younger castmate had left her worse off than ever. The ensuing mid-tour breakup made for awkwardness of unparalleled magnitude. She finished that tour to come home to some family difficulties that propelled her right back onto the road in *The Show About the Rat.*

Rabbit knew she was not in the best emotional place. But none of the self-help books she devoured, or the positive affirmations she affirmed, or the yoga she... yoga'd... seemed to be of any benefit.

(As a side note, Rabbit was a certified yoga instructor. The more certified yoga instructors I meet, the more I believe that there must be some kind of required degree of emotional instability before they certify you. Like Mensa for crazy people.)

Anyway, Rabbit got worse and worse as each day of this particularly gruelling tour passed. I've complained about *The Show About the Rat* already. It was a miserable experience even for those of us in usually healthy mental states. Rabbit had a rabid hatred towards our marathon sessions of van Trivial Pursuit. It wasn't because the game was particularly rowdy or disruptive that she hated it. It was because we were enjoying ourselves so much on what should have been miserable drive days.

Rabbit got worse and worse until our final show in Moose Jaw, Saskatchewan[10] where she disappeared in the middle of the performance. She wasn't in the wings. She wasn't in the dressing room. She wasn't in the green room.

Those of us who'd been tracking her emotional descent thought she'd finally snapped. Some thought she must have gone to

---

9 Show + Romance = Showmance. A "don't poop where you eat" situation if ever there was one.

10 Which is coincidentally my hometown. If you're ever driving across the Canadian prairies, check out our giant moose statue. City officials decided to remove the statue's testicles after vandals kept painting them green.

her dressing room after her previous scene, packed up her costume and just taken off. But her bags and street clothes were all there.

And that's when I got really worried. A part of me knew that she hadn't gone that far—that a person wouldn't up and kill themselves in the middle of a kid's show. Maybe in the middle of a Chekhov. After all, most of the characters kill themselves by the end—and that's in his comedies. But surely not in *The Show About the Rat*.

But there was still a nagging doubt. The second the curtain dropped for intermission, I ran through all the bathrooms and storage rooms and rehearsal halls in the basement of the theatre. But she was nowhere to be found.

The cast quickly put together some contingency plans for the second act—re-blocking songs and reassigning lines of dialogue, while I, with my basically non-existent role, continued scouring the building. It was in my third sweep of the basement that I heard a faint knocking at a door that lead to a stairway fire exit from the basement.

Poor Rabbit had not snapped. She'd merely zigged where she should have zagged.

The theatre had no backstage crossover. So if you exited stage left and needed to re-enter stage right, you had to go down some stairs through a labyrinthine basement, then back up to stage level. Rabbit took a wrong turn and ended up on the wrong side of a locked fire escape door. The only way she could have gotten herself backstage from there would have been to go out the fire escape, around the block to the rear of the theatre and into the stage door. As all she was wearing was a black unitard, and as it was minus ten billion degrees outside, the average temperature in Saskatchewan in February, this was not a viable option.

Up until Rabbit's Moose Javian vanishing act, most of the cast had grown pretty dismissive of her perpetual gloom. Throughout the tour we complained to each other that she just needed to cheer up. I spent our European tour actively avoiding having to deal with her. I was annoyed with people who I saw as "coddling" or "enabling" her.

It was only when I feared she may have gone over the edge that I realized what a judgemental asshole I'd been. Over the years I've had my share of failures and frustrations. I know you can't just cheer up. You need someone to love and support you, while at the same time challenging you not to wallow in your own misery. You need to know someone pretty well to walk this fine line, to love without coddling and challenge without judging, and I never bothered to get to know Rabbit well enough to do that.

That was Rabbit's final tour, thank God. In the intervening two years, I have heard reports, which I sincerely hope are accurate, that she is in a much better place. I'm just glad she waited at that door for someone to find her. She probably would have frozen to death before she made it to the stage door. And freezing to death in a black unitard on the streets of Moose Jaw, Saskatchewan is an unacceptable way for any human being to die.

LAME BUS/PARTY BUS

I don't remember what I was dreaming about before we stopped for gas in the middle of the night somewhere between Strasbourg and Grenoble, France. I do remember how my dream ended. We were surrounded by zombies who kept repeating the name "Angelaaaaa, Angelaaaaa, Angelaaaaa" in the same gravelly, slurred tone they normally use moaning for braaaaaaains.

When I awoke I realized that, though the zombies were an invention of my unconscious mind, the voices calling for Angelaaaaa were not. Our incredibly drunk French road manager Luc had stumbled from the crew bus onto ours, looking for Angela, a British former Lido dancer whose job on our tour I'm still at a loss to define. The crew was having a party on their bus—as they did on every overnight drive—and they wanted us to join them.

The producers had arranged for us to travel in large touring buses, with bunks on the upper level and living room-style seating on the bottom level. Two out of three nights we stayed in hotels. But many nights we had to drive from one end of France to the other to make it in time for the show the next day. We crisscrossed the country so many times it was like who ever built the show itinerary just threw darts at a map of France blindfolded.

The crew loved the overnight drives. Every time the buses would make a pit stop, they would stagger, drunk and singing, out of their bus, great clouds of cigarette smoke billowing out after them. They needed no excuse to drink, and did so constantly. When we first met up with the crew in Montpellier, they were offended that we wouldn't drink wine with our lunch – despite the fact that we had to do three shows immediately afterward. Work obligations didn't stop them from partaking, why should it stop us?

Hours later that same night, following another stop, I was awoken by the sound of the most extreme snoring I've ever heard. One of the French crewmen, who had hooked up with one of the female members of the cast, had drunkenly stumbled into her bunk and joined her there. At first I was relieved that he'd just fallen asleep, but I eventually realized that the sound of copulation would have been much preferable to the ungodly noises coming out of his sinuses.

It was like there was a lumber mill operating inside his face, and there was nothing I could do to make it stop. At one point, I threw a copy of the Complete Works of William Shakespeare at him. But the collected force of some fifteen hundred pages of English's greatest author was powerless to stop the common French snore. Maybe it's because of the nasal placement with which French people talk (as compared to the more guttural Quebecois French with which I'm more familiar) that made him such an effective snorer. Maybe he had a horrible sinus infection. Maybe he took special lessons. I don't know. All I know is that I did not sleep any more that night.

Upon arriving at our theatre in Grenoble, the crew, in conditions ranging from hungover to still drunk, were already setting up the temporary stage and thousands of pounds audio gear and lighting rigging—a not so comforting thought given that failure to properly secure a lighting truss could result in a lot of dead people in animal costumes.

But that was just an average night for the crew. They were more used to working drunk and hungover than clear-headed. Finish the show, pack up the set, get blackout drunk on the bus, sleep for three hours, then set up the next show. Finish the show, pack up the set, get blackout drunk, etc, etc... Contrast that with the cast. Finish the show, have a glass of wine on the bus followed by an OFFICIALLY MANDATED PROHIBITION ON NOISE STRICTLY ENFORCED AT ELEVEN PM. Those cast members who enjoyed partying did so on the crew bus, and even then, only sparingly.

For a while, I was amazed at our French crew's ability to maintain that kind of gruelling schedule over the long haul. Most of them were drunk for the entire tour—as soon as they started sobering up it was lunchtime, and in France one does not eat lunch without a glass (or three) of wine. It wasn't until one of my castmates walked by the production office and found a bunch of them snorting some magical nose dust that we learned how they managed to get through the day.

The crew thought we were pretty lame, which I can understand. As my French is embarrassingly poor, I didn't spend a lot of time talking to the crew. But from what I heard, they were used to touring with French rock acts—who were more amenable to the party life than children's entertainers. We had a few crew/cast parties along the way, but even the tamest among the crew would get drunker and stay later than any of us. I think a younger cast would have tried harder to keep up. But everyone in the cast was between their late twenties and early thirties—the time you start realizing you can't pull all-nighters and function the next day like you did in college. Staying up that way leaves me feeling foggy for at least two days now.

The ironic thing is that our much harder-living crew skewed

older—most in their mid 30's to 40's. Some were single, but many had girlfriends or wives. Some even had kids. But for all of them working as road crew wasn't just a fun thing to do for a while. It wasn't a neat break from the cycle of auditioning and working your way through regional theatres the way it was for us. It was their career. It was their identity. Where the cast was a bunch of actors drawn from across Canada, doing a single contract before moving on to the next gig, the crew identified as a band of brothers. The crew coped with the costs of a permanently itinerant life by drinking themselves stupid every night. If I knew I wouldn't be seeing my child in months, I might do the same.

The drinking and smoking were the biggest culture shocks for the cast. Some people have a perception of actors as alcohol-fueled train wrecks, but my experience has shown that simply isn't the case. Especially with Canadian actors. People tend to be much more concerned about protecting their voices and staying in good health until the end of the run. We're too used to working with no understudies. You don't get to take a show off unless you're dead, and even then the assistant stage manager might prop your corpse up on a dolly and roll you around the stage, reading your lines from a script.

Nobody wants to have to do a show sick, particularly a show in those big animal costumes. Doing a show hung over in a massive, furry, sweat drenched bear costume, where the only thing you can smell are your own farts, breath, and body odour would be a special kind of hell.

SQUISHED FOX

It was the middle of December and Toulouse was hot. Not unseasonably hot, but having grown up in the Canadian prairies, I find the absence of snow and freezing winds and the unnatural juxtaposition of Christmas trees and palm trees disturbing. The missus and I spent the day exploring the city and admiring the pink brick buildings that dominate Toulouse's architecture. I sweated through my shirt and stuffed as much Basque lamb stew into my face as my stomach would tolerate. The missus kept her eyes peeled for a Nespresso store to score some free coffee. It was a pretty average day for us on our European tour of *The Turtle Show*.

But when we arrived back at the theatre for the show, we discovered that Fox had been hit by a car.

Fox was a contemporary dancer from Montreal, artistically slumming it doing children's theatre to save up money to fund more fulfilling projects with her own dance company. She was tall and thin and brought a grace to the mascot work I've yet to see anyone else live up to. The show was really a waste of her exceptional talent. I just waved my arms and jumped around a lot.

I think it says something about how working in the theatre wrecks your brain that the first thing I thought when I heard the news was not "I hope she's okay," but "what are we going to do about the show?" Most big shows have at least one understudy per major role and a few ensemble members who can swing into any other ensemble track in case of sickness. Smaller shows simply cannot afford that luxury, and producers are left to pray that nobody in the cast spontaneously combusts.

I've spent most of my career working for the kinds of theatres that need you to go on, no matter how sick you are. I once did a show where one of the actors performed with such a violent stomach flu that the crew were positioned in each wing with buckets and he wore adult diapers under his costume—just in case. We re-blocked as much of his part as we could—get him onstage later, get him offstage sooner, cut anything that required him to run or jump. In the end, we all survived the ordeal. He made liberal use of the buckets throughout the show, but thankfully never needed the diapers.

While working as a singer on a cruise ship, we would only cancel shows in the very worst of storms – the kind of storms that turned all two thousand eight hundred passengers and crew from human beings into green vomit machines. Even at the best of times, the dancers had to do lifts, pirouettes, and jumps on a constantly moving stage as we sailed from Caribbean island to Caribbean island. We had to re-block the show on an almost weekly basis to accommodate whatever fresh injuries to ankles, knees, and backs the dancers had sustained that week.

Sometimes there are medical emergencies that even the most dedicated of actors can't power through. When one of the actors I'd hired in a show I'd written and self-produced called to tell me he had a blood clot in his leg and could die if he left the hospital, I went on for him with the script attached to a clipboard. The other actors would guide me around the stage, or feed me lines when we got lost.

By the time Fox was hit by a car in Toulouse, I was a little bit too used to troubleshooting cast injuries and illness.

While we didn't have an understudy for Fox, we did have two different actors playing Turtle. The Turtle costume was so hard on the performer's neck, and the Turtle role was so exhausting, that the company had decided to have two actresses alternate days—playing Turtle one day, puppeteering the next. The puppeteering track required a minimal amount of physical energy, and almost zero concentration. If they hadn't split the Turtle track they way they had, whoever would have been just been the puppeteer would have almost certainly developed the Stump Complex.

So it was decided that one of the Turtles would go in for Fox and our hapless road manager was roped into puppeteering. Unfortunately, the Turtle costume was designed for someone five feet tall and Fox was designed for someone almost six feet. The Turtle who bravely volunteered to fill in for Fox was none other than my missus, who claims to be five feet tall, but is really closer to four-eleven. The way the fabric of the costume bunched up made it look like Fox had been squished like an accordion.

By the time everyone was back at the theatre from their daily adventures, we only had around thirty minutes to rehearse the dance numbers with our makeshift squished Fox. All the voices for the mascot characters were pre-recorded voice over, so we didn't have to worry about her forgetting lines or lyrics. Even so, we didn't even have time to get to most of the songs by the time the show started. Anytime Squished Fox wandered off in the wrong direction, someone would shove her where she was supposed to go. Anytime Squished Fox didn't know what dance move she was supposed to do, she just busted out some sweet free-styling.

We survived the show and, it is hoped, the audience was unaware that anything was wrong. If a parent noticed Fox looked a little like a deflated balloon, or seemed to not know where she was going half the time, I'm sure the five year old they were with was too excited to notice. Normal Fox returned from the hospital that night with, miraculously, only minor bumps and bruises. Nothing broken, no concussion. Though sore and achy, she was well enough to do the show the next day.

The unpredictability of live-theatre—the fact that at any time, something horrible can go wrong—is one of the things that make it so rewarding both to be part of and to watch. When I stepped in for the actor who had a blood clot in his leg, we explained to the audience what was going on—and offered them free tickets to any future performance so they could see the show with the original cast. It ended up being one of our most vocally appreciative audiences. Any time I couldn't find my place in the script, or started exiting in the wrong direction and had to be shoved towards the opposite wing by my castmates, they would erupt in laughter and applause.

Over the years, I've started looking forward to things going wrong in shows. Having someone rescue you when you drop a line, or having someone who can improvise with you when someone misses an entrance, or a phone doesn't ring, or a light doesn't turn on, or a curtain doesn't close, or a prop breaks teaches you who you can trust better than a million perfectly executed performances. Some actors are unresourceful in the face of adversity. Some are too selfish or lazy to bother trying to keep things moving. But there is nothing more satisfying than discovering you're working with the kind of people who would keep the show going regardless of nuclear holocaust, zombie apocalypse, or the fact that they have such bad diarrhoea that they have to wear an adult diaper in case they crap themselves.

SPACE INVADER SAFARI

As our tour of French speaking Europe progressed it became increasingly clear that the show was hemorrhaging money. The producer reduced the quality of our hotels from sumptuous in city centres to seedy on city outskirts. While doing a show in Geneva, our hotel was so far out of town that it wasn't even in Switzerland. Our hotel breakfasts went from fresh baked pastry, rich cheeses, and lavish charcuterie spreads to stale baguette, stale baguette, and stale baguette.

Me and the missus could hardly pack a decent lunch and supper from such a meagre breakfast spread![11]

The show's financial demise rested on our producer's decision to run the show for three weeks in Paris. If we'd only toured the provinces, the show would have been profitable. The producer had no trouble selling out a two-thousand-seat theatre for three shows in Lyon, Montpellier, or Rouen. But he couldn't get more than three hundred for any of the thirty shows we did in Paris. I don't know why he wanted to crack Paris so bad—maybe it's a prestige

11 Have I mentioned we're cheap?

thing.

From that point on we spent every day off in Paris—even if it meant a twelve-hour drive from the opposite end of the country. Almost everyone on the crew was Parisian, and the cost of fuel to drive back to Paris was cheaper than hotel rooms for the entire crew. The cast was dumped in the cheapest hotel the producer could find—on the freeway, far from the City of Light.

But hey, we were still in Paris, right? It's not like we were in Fort Mcmurray in February, or (shudder) Fresno, at any time of the year.

I'm not sure if this is true of the rest of humanity, but if you put a bunch of actors together in the kind of situation they otherwise would only have dreamed of ever attaining, a perfect storm of lots of money, lots of time off, lots of good food, lots of good people to share it with, and all this in the one of the most beautiful places on Earth, they will inevitably find something to complain about.

I once heard one of my cast mates complain that he was sick of all the old buildings in Paris. And this chap was from Winnipeg of all places. *Winnipeg.* The home of frostbite and sadness and stabbings. I heard another complain about the catering we ate at each theatre—which, in order to keep the French crew from mutinying, was always of exceptional quality.[12] His ideal day involved searching whatever town we were in for their local McDonalds.

Our new, terrible hotel's distance from the city centre, combined with having already spent close to a month in Paris, meant that some of the cast opted just to watch movies on their laptops at the hotel and eat at a nearby mall food court (which

---

12 With the notable exception of a town called Bressuire in which we were served an oily black stew containing meat and sausage from any animal they could get their hands on, served from a trough. I shit thee not. A trough. I called it the Bucket o' Meat. Oh, and we were also served pigeon once. That was disgusting too, although the crew certainly seemed to love it.

included a McDonalds THANK GOD FOR THAT).

But the missus and I were determined to make the most out of our time in France. At first we tried walking into town from the hotel—which the hotel's concierge assured us was impossible. We'd heard that nonsense before. People don't realize how intrepid urban explorers like us can walk from anywhere. But after almost dying on the shoulder of Paris's freeways, we had to begrudgingly concede defeat. The city was literally inaccessible by foot from our hotel. Freeways hemmed it in on all sides.

We eventually found a bus that weaved its way through the Parisian suburbs, which connect to the end of one of Paris's subway lines. Only ninety-minutes later, we were downtown. But what to do? We'd already been to all the major attractions—I wasn't counting on being back in Paris, so I'd made sure to ram in as much as I could during our first three weeks. And my wife assured me she would no longer be my wife if we spent any more time in museums.

Weeks earlier, while on a free walking tour I spotted a small tile mosaic of a Pac-Man ghost cemented onto the side of a building. Our guide explained that it was put there by a Parisian street artist named Space Invader, who had hundreds of similar pieces scattered around the city. After doing a little research into Space Invader, I found a map that a fan had made listing the location of every piece that this very prolific street artist had installed. I copied the locations down onto our street atlas and set about finding and documenting as many as we could in our two days off.

The Space Invader Safari was born.

The first one to spot the mosaic scored a point and had their picture taken beside it. Every couple hours we'd stop at a park and eat some of our stale breakfast baguette. When we got sick of that, we'd get some olives, cheese, salad and a mini-bottle of red wine from a grocery store.

Over the course of those two days, we spent twenty-four hours roaming the streets of Paris. We probably covered close to a hundred and twenty kilometres distance, up and down magnificent boulevards and little side streets. We ended up finding eighty of the mosaics, I spotted forty four, the missus thirty six.[13]

It's funny to me that despite going to such icons as the Eiffel Tower, Montmartre, the Pompidou, Palais Garnier, or to the Louvre (three times) what I remember best, and most fondly, are those two days wandering the streets, hunting for tile mosaics of video game characters from my childhood. Up to that point I felt like a tourist doing things, surrounded by other tourists in one of the most touristy cities in the world. Somehow the Space Invader Safari made Paris feel like it was mine. And though my French remains embarrassingly bad, it made me feel a little bit like an insider.

The only picture on the wall in my home-office is a photo of one of the Space Invader mosaics in Paris. It serves as a valuable reminder that the best way to experience life is to get out there, make it your own, and do it until blisters bleed through your socks. There aren't enough Big Macs in all the MacDonalds in all the world I would have traded those days for.

---

13 I am a CHAMPION!!!!!

THE MISSUS

Over a year ago The Children's Theatre Company won the rights to a very popular pre-teen girl-oriented cartoon, which for the sake of this article we'll call *The Fruit Show*. The show promised to be a good one—the music was slick and well-produced, and the script was actually more or less coherent. But the best part was that none of the characters were mascots – nobody in the show would have to go into a head. Almost every woman on the company's roster of performers desperately wanted to go on this tour, including my wife.

The clients who own the rights to the characters being portrayed (usually an animation production company) are very strict about how the characters look. With the mascots, the battles were fought over costume design. In *The Show About The Rat* the clients had a big problem with the fact that Cat's mouth was open as it rarely opens its mouth in the cartoon. But in order for the actor to be able to make it through the show without killing everyone else on stage, there needed to be an opening for him to see through. Eventually the client let it go, but it was a near thing.

They don't care what the person inside the costume looks like, as long as the costume fits. In *The Turtle Show*, Fox, a male character, was played by a woman, and Beaver, a female character, was played by a man.

The three questions any director/producer has to ask when casting a show is: Do they look right? Are they skilled enough? And what are they going to be like to work with?—usually in that order. Not worrying about someone's look being accurate has lead The Children's Theatre Company to a very informal casting process—usually based entirely on recommendations of current cast members rather than auditions. But because none of the licensed characters in *The Fruit Show* were in mascot costumes, the company was forced to have a much more normal casting process, (i.e., actually audition people).

The missus auditioned in early 2012. She was always a favourite of the powers that be in the company, so she was presented to the clients as a potential candidate for one of the characters. After much back and forth they eventually rejected her for the role. The missus was devastated. She was instead offered a role on the inexplicably popular *The Show About the Rat*, which was being sent out for its third tour—this time of Western Canada. As we're both from Western Canada, the itinerary wasn't exotic. As she'd already done the show, the show wasn't novel. There was little appealing about the tour, but she decided to take it anyway—it was going to be her last hurrah with The Children's Theatre Company. Her plan was to transition from the world of performing to the behind the scenes world of casting, a move that would provide us with enough stability to eventually start a family.

But then, a few weeks after *The Show About the Rat* ended, after she'd already started a job at with a Toronto casting director, she received an email notifying her that the clients had changed their minds, and that she was booked for the four month tour of *The Fruit Show*.

So off she went for another four months on the road. She spent six of the nine months between September and May of this year touring, a particularly gruelling time of separation that I've briefly mentioned already.

It kind of made me hope that I die before she does. Things got real boring without my partner in crime. I had a hard time making plans with people—I'm too used to just saying "what do you want to do tonight?" then going out and doing it. I'd forget to plan ahead, find out all my friends already had plans, then have nothing to do. To make matters worse, in terms of my social life, I had received a rather large grant to write a musical adaptation of a well-known Canadian novel. I worked from home, by myself. And at the end of the day, I had no plans. At least if I'd still been working at a restaurant to pay the bills, I would have had work-colleagues to hang out with after a shift. I ended up just playing a lot of video games.

The only thing I liked about the missus being away was that the toothpaste was always squeezed from the bottom and the cap was always screwed on.

But we've been very lucky to have had many opportunities to work together as well. We've done a total of five contracts together over the years, four of them tours. When we toured together we spent almost every minute of every day together. We shared a hotel room and a dressing room at the theatre. We sat next to each other in the van and would spend our free time exploring whatever city we were in.

And during those months that we spent every waking minute together, I never once wished that I could have a little time away from her. That's not to say we don't drive each other crazy sometimes – the aforementioned toothpaste remains a bone of contention—but there is no one else I would rather have drive me crazy.

She's excessive in the extreme—while in a Wal-Mart

somewhere in New England, she found some gas pills on sale for negative seventeen cents (on sale for $1.83, plus a flier coupon for $2 off). Rather than buy a normal amount of gas pills a person might conceivably need over the course of a lifespan, she bought ALLOF THEM, using them to offset the cost of some expensive make-up. Seriously, if you ever find yourself bloated and gassy in Toronto, stop by. I will hook you up.

On *The Fruit Show* she crossed back and forth over the Canada/US border three times. As alcohol is considerably cheaper in the US, she bought as much booze, wine, or beer they'd let her. If anyone in the cast were not buying duty-free, she'd get more, and make them claim it for her. After her tour we needed a grocery cart to wheel it all up from the lobby. Seriously, if you ever find yourself sober in Toronto, stop by. I will hook you up.

When she got back to Toronto, she couldn't just have one job. She started to worry she wouldn't be busy enough and looked for others until she had one thousand jobs. One week last month she worked a total of eighty hours, in several different jobs. The complicated schedule juggling required to make this possible would have given me an ulcer. I've managed to talk her down to two jobs —working at the casting director's office during the week, and bartending ONE NIGHT per weekend. Seriously, if you're ever in Toronto and need a job doing promotions, or bartending, or running an audition session, stop by. I will hook you up.

But this excessive behaviour also impacts how she cares about the people around her. She remembers everything everyone ever says to her, which means she remembers when someone says they like something or need something—making her the best at buying presents. She will do anything to help a friend—and you really have to be a special kind of asshole in order for you to not be her friend.

She calls me out for being self-righteous or when I'm full of some other variety of balogna. She completely believes in my talents, and is a hundred percent supportive of my writing. She keeps me honest about how hard working I am—because really, when you are a freelance writer, it's very easy to spend a couple hours making good progress on a piece, then pat yourself on the back and call it a day. When I have to explain to someone who just finished a twelve-hour shift how I spent my day, it makes me want to at least come close to matching that amount of effort.

I've seen relationships I thought were solid crumble. It scares me to think how we might grow apart, or how radically different our life will be when we have a kid. I don't ever want to be that guy who goes to a bar to get away from his spouse. I always want to relish our time together, as I do now, and as I have for the last four years of our marriage. I just hope we can continue to grow together instead of growing apart...

Now if only we could do something about that toothpaste lid...

OUT OF THE HEAD

In January of 2008 I had just finished running *Funny Business,* a show in Toronto that I had written and self-produced, which, thanks to my stubborn belief that I could eventually get the damned thing profitable, I had kept running for five months, always putting any profits into advertising in order to keep it going rather than paying myself a producer's fee. For months I would go to work at a Starbucks from 5:30 AM until my day at my office at the theatre started at 10:30 AM, where I would work on producer-y jobs until show time, during which I was the assistant stage manager. After the show I would stand outside the large scale musicals, like *Dirty Dancing, The Drowsy Chaperone,* and *We Will Rock You,* to hand out fliers to the people leaving the theatre —usually getting home by 11:30 PM. Then, I'd get up at 4:00 AM to start the whole thing again: work for nine dollars an hour and get yelled at by rich douches because their cappuccino wasn't dry enough, then back to the theatre to sign over eight thousand dollars worth of payroll cheques to my cast, who would then yell at me because the theatre was too cold. Or too hot. Or because the pianist played the tempos too slow. Or too fast. By the end of the ordeal I was utterly exhausted and broke.

The day after we closed I flew to my parents' home in Saskatchewan to rest and lick my wounds, only to discover my dad had just been diagnosed with terminal cancer. I spent the next half year doing my best to care for my mom while she cared for my dad before he passed away in June. By the end of this ordeal I was utterly exhausted, broke, and broken.

I spent that summer in Dawson City, Yukon, singing in a Klondike gold-rush era revue show that ran in a casino/tourist trap. At the end of the summer, I found myself at a crossroads. I had all of my worldly possessions with me in two suitcases. I felt very little calling me back to Toronto, the city that I felt I had been utterly defeated by. But I didn't feel compelled to go anywhere else. Move to Vancouver? Meh. Calgary, Edmonton, Winnipeg? Meh. Move south to the States? Meh. Move back to Saskatchewan, go to University and start over? Meh.

It was then that the previous Bear backed out of a tour that my then girlfriend (and future missus) was about to start.

"Should I push them to hire you?" she'd asked.

Meh.

But she pushed anyway, and the next thing I knew I was on a plane back to Toronto for rehearsals.

Two weeks later, I stood backstage in a theatre in a town called Lloydminster, where this book began, wondering if I was going to make it through the show alive (and then almost nearly didn't). A week later I stood under the dominating majesty of the Rocky Mountains. A week later, I ate as much seafood during the West Coast swing as my stomach could tolerate. A week later, I was surrounded by Redwoods outside of San Francisco. A week later, the garish lights and incessant noise on the Vegas strip nearly induced a seizure (and a Russian pet circus nearly induced vomiting). A week later, I witnessed the much more spectacular lighting display of the stars in the endless skies of the prairie at night.

Then, a week later, I was back in Toronto, once again looking forward to life and optimistic about the future.

In many ways I'm still recovering from the ordeals of late 2007 through mid 2008. Every night for months after my father's death, I would dream that he was still alive. I now only have these dreams once or twice a month. For months after *Funny Business* closed all I could talk about was the bitterness of employing my friends only for them to decide that they hated my guts the second I cut them their first check. Now I have an easier time remembering all the hilarious antics that went down on stage and off. But I'm more anxious than I used to be. More indecisive. And much more introverted.

But I don't know where or what I'd be now if I didn't have that opportunity to run away with the circus for a while. I had seriously considered giving up entirely. When you wear one of those mascot costumes you can only see through a small, mesh covered hole, usually in the character's open mouth. Everything around you fades. The only thing that matters is what is directly in front of you. When you tour your daily needs of food and shelter are arranged by your road manager. All you have to do is show up.

If you've reached the point where you can't process your life beyond the present moment, there might be no better place to recover than inside a bear's head.

Since then, I've been on three more tours. I've seen most of North America and Western and Central Europe. But my last tour was now two years ago. I've gone from being utterly hopeless about my future to so excited about everything I'm doing in Toronto that I'm loathe to leave for too long.

I'm grateful for having learned about and experienced the Stump Complex, and how to cook in hotel rooms; for learning to live in the moment from Bird, empathy from Rabbit, perseverance from Fox, patience from crazy parents, and economics from merch markups; for small miracles in Marseilles, for the hours and hours of Trivial Pursuit, for the months spent trekking across Europe looking for eight-bit tile mosaics with the Missus.

But I'm most glad that, after that first show, I was always able to find my way offstage without accidentally stage diving onto a bunch of five year olds.

ABOUT THE AUTHOR

(this guy)

Daniel Falk is a writer/actor/player-of-video-games based in Toronto. He has been a regular contributor to *McSweeney's Internet Tendency* and *The Big Jewel*. In 2007 he produced his co-written musical *Funny Business* which ran for five months in Toronto and provided him the valuable life lesson that producing theatre in Canada isn't so much a career as it is a very expensive hobby. He lives in a cube of air with his wife(sorry ladies), their invisible pet mongoose Robocop, and their zero beautiful children.

You can reach Daniel for questions, comments, or relationship advice at:

Email – thegreatrobot@gmail.com
Twitter – @thegreatrobot
Website – www.thegreatrobot.com
Smashwords – www.smashwords.com/profile/view/thegreatrobot

Or by shouting really really really loudly.

92119621 A